Black Tupelo Country

Black Tupelo Country

Doug Ramspeck

Winner of the John Ciardi Prize for Poetry
Selected by Leslie Adrienne Miller

BkMk Press
University of Missouri-Kansas City

BkMk Press
University of Missouri-Kansas City
5101 Rockhill Road
Kansas City, Missouri 64110
(816) 235-2558 (voice) / (816) 235-2611 (fax)
www.umkc.edu/bkmk

Cover design: Ryan MacDonald
Author photo: Michael J. Ayers
Book interior design: Susan L. Schurman
Managing Editor: Ben Furnish
Associate Editor: Michelle Boisseau
BkMk Press wishes to thank Nathan Becka, Elizabeth Gromling, Cara
Lefebvre, and Gina Padberg.

.

The John Ciardi Prize for Poetry wishes to thank Lindsay Martin Bowen,
Susan Cobin, Greg Field, Steve Gehrke, Nadine Meyer,
Maryfrances Wagner, and Sam Witt.

Library of Congress Cataloging-in-Publication Data

Ramspeck, Doug

Black tupelo country : poems / Doug Ramspeck.
    p. cm.
"Winner of the John Ciardi Prize for Poetry selected by Leslie Adrienne
Miller."
    Summary: "Black Tupelo Country, a poetry collection, explores the
themes of animism, superstition, and anachronism as they occur in rural
Midwestern landscapes and urban strip malls. Many poems explore how
the natural and supernatural worlds interconnect in language and percep-
tion, and the human tendency to read nature into fears and longings"--
Provided by publisher.
    ISBN 978-1-886157-65-1 (pbk. : alk. paper)
    I. Title.

PS3618.A479B63 2008
811'.6--dc22

                                    2008044434

This book is set in BiauKai, Century Gothic, and Cochin.
Printed on recycled paper by Walsworth Publishing Company, Marceline, Missouri.

Acknowledgments

Grateful acknowledgment is made to the editors of the following publications where the poems in this collection first appeared:

Blue Unicorn: "Swamp Wedding."
The Bryant Literary Review: "The Covenant."
California Quarterly: "The Known World."
Chautauqua Literary Journal: "Horse, Meadow, Horse."
The Cream City Review: "Retirement Years."
Cider Press Review: "Entropy" and "Magnolia."
Cold Mountain Review: "Confetti."
Confrontation Magazine: "Winter Ash."
Connecticut Review: "Original Woods" and "The Veil."
Crab Orchard Review: "Bottomlands Memory, 1927."
DMQ Review: "Ritual Cloud Line."
The Evansville Review: "Epistemology in Cleveland."
Fugue: "Hillside Wraith."
The Gihon River Review: "Wild Dogs."
Good Foot: "No Other Sign."
Green Hills Literary Lantern: "Where We Come From."
Harpur Palate: "Sunday Mornings" and "Black Tupelo Country."
Hubbub: "Provenance."
Illuminations: An International Magazine of Contemporary Writing: "The Myth of Ice."
Knock: "Dressing the Dead."
Lake Effect: A Literary Journal of the Arts: "The Lake Beneath the Sky," "Weed Song," and "Here Is What I Know about the Sky."
Louisiana Literature: "The Offering."
Madison Review: "Speaking of Rivers."
The Mid-America Poetry Review: "Rockmilk."
Natural Bridge: "The Water in Between."
Nimrod International Journal: "Ice Junco" and "Ouroboros."
Parting Gifts: "Disfigured Night" and "Stationary Darkness."
Passages North: "Blue Toaster."
Pebble Lake Review: "Distant Trees" and "The Marriage."
Pennsylvania English: "Symmetry" and "Bird, Branch."
Permafrost: "Indifferent Light."
Poem: "Teaching the Gods to Breathe."
Rattle: "Bottomlands Widow."
River Oak Review: "Black Water."
Roanoke Review: "Afterglow" and "Beneath the Shagbark."
Rhino: The Poetry Forum: "Visiting Hours."

Rosebud: "Simulacrum."
Seneca Review: "Foreshortened."
Slant: "Desire."
South Dakota Review: "July Drought as Harbinger of Plenty."
The Sow's Ear Poetry Review: "Eventide."
The Strange Fruit: "The Return."
West Branch: "Four Hooves and the Goat to Go with Them" and "Full
        Circle."
Willow Review: "Quarry Lake."

The author wishes to thank Leslie Adrenne Miller, Ben Furnish,
Michelle Boisseau, Ryan MacDonald, and Vivian Shipley.

For Beth and Lee

Black Tupelo Country

V

VI

VII

VIII

IX

X

XI

Foreword

Erst in dem Doppelbereich
werden die Stimmen
ewig und mild.

—Rilke, *Sonnets to Orpheus* (I, 9)

*B*lack Tupelo Country is a book of cinematic lushness razored
with ache. These poems dwell in the dark, mutable seam
between the natural and interior worlds. "Covenant," the
book's first poem, is exactly that, a contract with the reader to fol-
low the writer into that indeterminate place between earth and self:
"because a woman's body is a prophet,/ she sleeps shivering by her
husband in July" and dreams of a massasauga snake that will slip in
and out of the rest of the book in many guises. When she rises she
sees "our covenant," our contract with our own mortality, figured as a
"bitch" alternately licking her pup and snarling. Here then is where
we begin: stepping in on a world at once familiar and mythical, par-
ticulate, real, deeply snarled in the flora and fauna of language itself:
"In mating season, these nouns/ can't tell themselves from verbs"
("Horse, Meadow, Horse").

It is not a book one can sample, but must be taken in all at once,
a Faulknerian saga of sensation and feeling rather than event. Once
we are in its world, we want to stay, hold our breath, ride the surprise
and suspense, the luxuriant images, waiting, as great novels make
one do, for revelation or destruction, because we so trust this voice,
the wholeness of the vision it lays out for us one shimmering incre-
ment at a time. The poet skillfully builds each successive poem from
some fragment of a previous lyric: that massasauga snake reappears
as anaconda, ringneck, rattler, milk snake, cottonmouth. In "Four
Hooves and the Goat to Go With Them," Adam and Eve sell subma-
rine sandwiches at the mall, and Odysseus buys "a partial interest in
Cinnabon." Socrates dumpster dives outside a Wal-Mart in Cleve-
land, while Dr. Mengele, a Wal-Mart Greeter in Miami, reads *The
Aeneid* evenings and buys a blue toaster with his employee discount.
These brilliant segues tease us toward the strange web of connection
between myth and word, earth and heart, land and human history
turned and shaped in the patterns of time and biology.

The poet's strategy is often to render a scene in precise, concrete
and hauntingly lyrical language, then to tinge it with menace: "Even

we ourselves are out to get us." Just when we think we've settled into a poem's conjuring of the gorgeous, something ominous slithers in, ineffable, inevitable, insinuating itself under and around the vision the poem is unfolding so we can hardly tell where it comes from or what it is, but again, the surety of the voice compels us into leaving what we recognize behind. These poems are impossible to parse because they bear out MacLeish's dictum that "a poem should not mean/ But be." They arrive in the mind like the "speleothems" in the poem "Rockmilk," "which thrive on one drip at a time."

The book's emotional arc plays out in eleven short sections that move us from shore to shore of lakes and rivers across the American Midwest—Ohio, Indiana, Michigan, Minnesota—and, deeper in, other rivers and continents, "Fulda River./ Saale, Ruwer, Volme," "Every river speaking in moans." Bodies of water are sites of memory and eternal present, places where language is found "loitering in bars. Words holy as pig manure on boot bottoms." It is this peculiar ability to exist, as Rilke suggests, in the *Doppelbereich*, the double realm, that makes this book so compelling, and so difficult to describe. Like Rilke's *Sonnets to Orpheus*, these poems probe that seam between realms/worlds/realities and allow us to glimpse what it might be like to dwell briefly in that between, though because we are human, mortal, of this earth, we cannot comprehend or hold that place for long in our imaginations. But reading Ramspeck's book lets us glimpse it, one moment, one poem, at a time,

> In the future pirouetting on the fang's edge
> or root-ravaged in the loam.
>
> All pouring from a burning
>   tupelo stump.
>
> (from "Ritual Cloud Line")

—Leslie Adrienne Miller
University of St. Thomas

I

The Covenant

Her flowers are dying in the old clay pot.
Her tomato vines are withering. The pact
she made was never with the dirt. At night
she dreams that the massasauga snake
leaves a final gift of skin beside the pond.
And the congealing waters—waters that offer
a catfish, belly up, floating in the shallows—
smell in summer like rotting, bestial flesh.
And because a woman's body is a prophet,
she sleeps shivering by her husband in July.
She would throw the bones and read them
if she could. She would twist her fingers
deep into the entrails. But for now she rises
in the dark and imagines expelling like a toad
a black and coiling string of eggs. Imagines
her breasts swollen, bloated with the milk.
Once she saw a mangy bitch nosing, nosing
at a pup. The pup's eyes were crusted shut.
This is our covenant. This is our covenant.
The bitch licked then snarled then licked.

July Drought as Harbinger of Plenty

The river is scorched as green.
Scorched as old men sitting on their porches.
Their hands slicing then reading the entrails
of catfish, five-lined skinks, voles.
While their wives, inside, mix potions:
milkwort, birdfoot trefoil, rattlebox, cow parsnip.
Potions watery as broth against the throat.
Then dusk arrives, releasing bats
waiting in the tupelos by shore.
Signaling us to climb from our windows
and walk the river's edge.
To summon love from the beer bottle neck.
To smell the river. To gather ourselves in the wire hair
of summer. In the augury of crayfish. To stand
on the bank where it hasn't rained for weeks.
Where dust lifts, hesitates, then falls.
Where once we found a massasauga skin and claimed
it as our own. Threw it as a harbinger into the river.
Where once we waded past the cattails, pressed our faces
in the muck. Swam.

Full Circle

It is quiet here. Like the penitent
returning to his knees or the dangling
blue fruit of the black tupelos.
If only memory hadn't silenced us
or we'd chosen the myth
of July winds coiling down
from the slope's lip, coiling
at day's end above the stream.
Beyond your shoulder the sky
is the color of a bruised peach,
and we listen for the oval leaves to start
to quiver. No wonder it has
come to this. We glance down
at the contagion of our hands.
The stream slips away between the rocks.
And all around, the black tupelos
are stretching out their limbs
as though to skewer us.

Afterglow

Everywhere was wreckage. A strange
premonitory wind blew down across
the poplars. This was no ceremonial
cleansing. We stopped our canoe
where the river had gnawed into the earth,
where charred roots twisted blackened
and exposed. Swollen sick, we walked
amid the ruins of dead trees. A lull
fell over us. We ourselves felt lightning struck—
as though the battered ghost or angry god
had us in mind. This, we knew, was not
ennobling suffering. Something crouched
and waited in the stillness. Something cried
out in the interrogator's voice.

Foreshortened

This, for instance, is the mustard-yellow memory of leaves. The
summer orchard where so many tumbled apples rot, ferment.
In my grandmother's parlor a massasauga snake skin hangs in
a reliquary beside the open window, and in my brother's attic
room, on the oak dresser, are the seeds of a hound's tongue and
a Culver's root wrapped twice then bound in motherwort.

It is dead hot in late July. The stains of sweat are pilgrim-sick
on rumpled sheets. At dawn I rise to see it: the river outside the
window foreshortened past the orchard. The gray lines narrowing
to meet.

Some mornings I awaken early to witness the night sky draining
away like an old-fashioned bloodletting. Soon my brother and I
will be smoldering in air. And we will walk into the ghost fruit,
into the rotting oracle. Our bare feet will soak up mush.

II

Horse, Meadow, Horse

It is as if, by climbing past the stream, we stumble
into something indeterminate.

Stumble into the unknown gray of dusk:
horses and meadow slipping into murkiness.

Slipping like something whispered in an ear.
Slipping like phonemes one against the other.

Look, you say. And at our feet
the dimming field edge defines itself as goldenrod.

And all around us is the grammar of the bobolink.
Each sudden, erratic diphthong. Each frenzied, reckless

morpheme. In mating season, these nouns
can't tell themselves from verbs.

So on we press into the twilight—
constructing this disassembling meadow.

And the horses, too. The smell of their warmth
sliding into tail-twitch sliding into whinny—

while night completes its slow declension, until all
that's left holding hands amid the bluestem is us.

Walking with these horses in our heads, with this meadow
on our tongue tips, with these wondrous firing neurons.

The Lake Beneath the Sky

Secret rivers hide on the lake bottom—
rivers no one sees, swirls and eddies
that lift the waves in silent chops. Above,
the lowering sky looks out on a countryside
stripped of green, harsh and ungodly in December.
We've made our camp on the rim of the world,
where sepulchral snows dissolve in placid water.
Supplicants of the lake, we do not trust the hills.
Earlier we crossed a stream moving across
a steady step of rocks, and you crossed
your arms over your ribs and turned away.
Now we sit beside the tent and wait for night.
The wind swirls down from the north, bringing
winter with it. Near shore are broken slabs
of ice, fat stone images, a nimbus of moonlight
pouring down the rocks. I've come to imagine
the struggle of water that takes place beneath
the lake in frozen weather—unseen currents
that collide with crystallizing liquid. It is water's way—
the silent battle beneath.

Winter Ash

Her artistry is like noon sunlight
in January skies. There is a pond
she used to skate on as a child—
blades carved out whatever
she once coveted. She speaks as though
she longs to feel her knees on stone,
to awaken in a monastery where
long robes are silent during prayer.
In Michigan tree twigs take on
slender coats of ice, and what waits
inside is in abeyance. At night
she sits out by her mulberries,
where nothing earthly intrudes
on falling snow. Passion, she says,
isn't swelling waves against rising
bows of boats, or lightning flashes
wild in August skies. It is January
darkness so alone it conjures white—
as though some celestial conflagration
falls as ash. Offering one hand
to the heavens, she grieves
joyfully that cold burns.

Magnolia

Neolecanium cornuparvum lay waste again this summer
to our magnolias. The tiny insects sucking
                                        sap, excreting
honeydew. Transmogrifying leaves
                                                to tar.
Around which nightly fireflies attempt to ford the
corporeal river.
                        There are no facts, only interpretations,
Nietzsche says—and so this year marks the third
that our interpretations thrive as nymphs in January,
turn translucent in the spring,
and give birth in late July.
                                        Our lives these days
are circumscribed by blight,
by the slow march of the unearthly feast
                                outside our bedroom window.
And some nights when we step into the garden—
as we watch our fireflies blink their way
                                        into the numinous,
as our shoes crunch against the fallen magnolia seed pods—
we interpret ourselves as answering some strange
                                        cathartic beckoning.
Interpret ourselves as part firefly,
                                part leaf.

III

The Veil

Fires rage all summer in these hills. We sleep,
we wake, the sun transforms our bodies in July.
Across the street the funeral home backs up
against the river. The trees aren't slick with moss
but dry, and even the loam around the river's edge
is parched. It is too hot for clothes. At night
the fires burn and we can see them. We feel awkward
in our skin. By day we contemplate the rigid faces
of the mourners—they stand dark and sluggish
by gleaming cars. The river moves. The smoke lifts
itself and veils the sky. We are moody in the heat
and wait for rain. We watch for wet leaves and bobbing
black umbrellas. Our voices are swollen as spring
rivers. We stand as supplicants before the glowing hills.

Original Woods

It feels familiar here. We recognize ourselves in
autumn leaves. Once we walked down this path
in moonlight—the rows of trees were windswept and
trembling as they undressed themselves. It is darker
beneath this canopy than we recall, the leafmeal a miasma
we've forgotten. Once again we plunge into ourselves—
sadness and pleasure cannot seem to tell themselves apart.
All morning we have been searching for the creek
we hope might offer us some comfort when we find it.
We understand that to live inside each other is to
scribble an essence we accept, to be carried upward
and to flutter in the wind. Our wish is to defy ourselves
and so take our rightful place amid the elements—
to fall back to earth and form this bed of leaves.

Simulacrum

This seems to be us sitting in a rowboat atop a June
wilderness of bay. We have stopped rowing. Each
green-gray wave lifts us in contemplation then lets go.
Earlier you sat in our bedroom window and watched
the sky above the fence. The squirrels were squabbling once
again in the back yard, chattering and chasing each other
in angry circles that fell forever back on themselves.
There is something wondrous in lighted surfaces, in prismatic
layers of brightness that understand the limits of illumination.
We negotiate our lives. What choice is there? The stairs
were loud as busybodies as I came up. You turned
and let your gaze surround me. The boat was in the bay beyond
your shoulder. The water swelled as if to swallow us.
Salt air poured through the screen in moist and restless waves.

Rockmilk

In rainless weather this streambed where we
go walking is dry mud. The ground beneath
our boots is leathery and cracked. I am new
to you these days. This is a losing stream, you
think, where whatever moisture gathers seeps
underground into the dolomite and marble.
But last March we ventured down into the cave
itself, where the warmer air was thick and damp.
Caves breathe. Cryptozoa hide beneath each stone;
dripholes sink down beneath your feet. And we
shone our flashlights on a copse of moonmilk—
as thick as paste, as wet as promise—and marveled
at phreatic water, which fills up the rock,
and speleothems, which thrive on one drip at a time.

IV

Where We Come From

Where we come from
we watch for quarter moons,
black blisterbeetles, cracks in glass,
discarded ringneck snake skins,
vespid wasp nests, pennywort,
split basswood trunks, short-tailed shrews.

Our memories are of brackish ponds
that dragged us once into the loam
and now bide their time and ache
to close around our mouths,
like a first love drawing us down
on rotted leaf mold.

Only fools trust the surface of a thing
like screech owls after midnight
or empty shadows of wormroot
or buried vole and bat bones
that grow a coven of stinkhorn mushrooms
which decay inside your nostrils as you breathe.

Even we ourselves are out to get us.
All our words are swampwater.
We sense each other in the buttonbushes,
we hear each fetid breath.
Our gnarled, sharpened talons are exposed
for when we swoop.

The Offering

The field came down last night
and opened like the walls of
a house when new and skeletal.
And since that's where I had
buried them, I spread a potion
of bitterweed and purple ruellias
above the ground. Some might
think I do not wish them happiness,
but in winter I sprinkle lactarii
and tricholomas across the field,
and in summer I grind up earwigs
and harvestmen as an offering.
She is not my wife these days,
but is, by right, remarried—
so she and her husband are serenaded
by the hoot owl's cry, and slither
joyfully with the milksnake in the grass.
After midnight I sometimes see them floating,
their moonlit skin as pale as stone.
And often in the summer—before
the corn comes down—the stalks
tremble in the wind, and I imagine
they are laughing in the grave.

Quarry Lake

This is a jimsonweed and dogbane kind of love,
a love like a five-lined skink inside a pocket.
We do not hold hands while we are walking;
we kiss only in the darkness of the quarry,
when the night weighs in like a toothache,
and the bats are rabid just above our heads.
Listen to the bullfrogs moan. A month ago
when we decided to get married, a hognose snake
crossed our path and hissed and lunged like a blessing.
Now we walk into the woods beside the quarry,
where paxilli grow, chanterelle, craterellus,
willow polypore, puffballs, stinkhorn, fairy butter.
You pick a baneberry and place it in my mouth.
I pick a baneberry and place it in yours.
This is our vow at Quarry Lake at dusk.

Wild Dogs

Something's wrong.
Bats dart amid the treetops.
Moonlight caresses the valley
in pale yellow. Come morning he watches
her slip into the bathtub.
Soap her skin with movements
slow as tides.

After breakfast she walks down
to her mother's cabin.
He sees them from the trees.
Sees them laugh and whisper on the porch.
Hears the whippoorwill conspiratorial
above him. Feels the sunlight
bear down in its betrayal.

Later she drives to the church cemetery
and walks out amid the tombstones.
A milk snake slithers past his feet.
Feral dogs begin coupling by the fence.
His eyes close and when he opens them
she has vanished.

That evening he concocts a potion of
pennywort, blue lupine, baneberry,
trumpet creeper. Stirs it in her
coffee after supper. Walks out
by the barn and buries one long

black hair in heavy loam.
Buries it with forest snails,
cankerworms, leafhoppers,
shaggy chanterelle.

And then that night he rolls over
in their bed to watch her breathe.
The rhythm doesn't quicken
as she sleeps. But then, much later,
she twitches like wild dreaming dogs—
and stands up suddenly.
Crosses to the window.
And lets moonlight
possess her.

Swamp Wedding

He vows to smother her with love.
There are black willows, possumhaw,
sweetbay, greater bladderwort, pickerelweed,
and Spanish moss. She lies to him
with seduction in her eyes. The swamp is rich
with wood ducks, prothonotary warblers,
sandhill cranes, pileated woodpeckers, white ibis.
Alligators sun themselves in sleepy bliss.
Green muck grows on the motionless river surface.
This is the smell of love. He knows it well.
He eyes her with suspicion. His tie constricts
his throat as the sun bears down. Her dress
is like the hypnotic white of the cottonmouth
before it strikes. The air is thick as sorrow.
The heat is dizzying. They are holding hands.
That night a barred owl will scream like it's been gutted.

Provenance

His earliest memories are of the shallow lake.
The heavy rotting smell of summer.
The cottonmouth's bloody fang marks on his knee.
When he was nine his sister drowned
enough she never was the same. Married
a farmer from Comal County, bore three sickly
children, died. When he was twelve
he made a bouquet of cattails, calamus,
flowering wapato—but the girl left him
on his own in the mesquite. There were times
he floated on his back in the shallow lake
and felt the heat foaming through his ribs.
He left for San Antonio at seventeen.
By nineteen he was back and fished
on Sundays. Each catfish fought and bled
as he dragged it from the shallows—each catfish
heaved and struggled in the dirt.

V

Visiting Hours

After their father died, the brothers imagined grief
pouring into the stream
behind the house. Its dull immensity
trickling with the green water
beyond the basswood trees.
Walking there, the brothers watched wild geraniums
claw from the earth by the railroad tracks.
Saw fluted swallowtails twitch like epileptics
near the barn. One night in August
a Norfolk Southern derailed
near the Mad River and for two days
not a single train shook the farmhouse
windows after midnight.
In the morning the brothers stepped outside
to see dust from the school bus float like a veil
across the scrub grass, and after dinner
a pale mist drifted down across the tickseed
and tried to smother it. That night
the younger brother dreamed
that death disguised itself as a young boy
while blood drops thumped like bruised plums
against the backyard grass. The older brother
dreamed he kissed his father's
rough cheek during Visiting Hours—
and what washed downstream derailed trains.

Entropy

It isn't so much what we felt, or didn't feel, or how we acted,
or didn't act—but like the space between heartbeats,
when nothing happens, when you are technically
alive but no blood pumps.

Mostly we are sitting, probably at school, and our math teacher
is talking about ordered pairs of integers, quadratic equations,
polynomials, algorithms. We are not daydreaming—
we have just shut down, though our eyes are nominally aware
of the fluorescent light above us faintly fluttering,
and maybe we feel hungry, but only as an afterthought,
as though it's not even our own stomachs that are growling.

And after school—you would think it would be different—
but we end up sitting in the basement of someone's house,
the music loud enough something almost seems to happen.
It throbs and throbs as though it wishes it could fill us.

Or we're out driving. Out into the countryside, the cornfields
flying by, perhaps to Raccoon Lake, where we sit by the shore
and smoke a cigarette and drink a beer. The black water is still
beneath the moonlight. We are still beneath the moonlight, too.
The stars are far away. They don't mean much. They stare at us
as we are staring back.

Indifferent Light

In this Indiana summer, tip blight turns
soybeans yellow. Sunlight settles
across flat prairie roads. We think
sometimes we are immune, as though
what lives inside us can't escape,
like wind blowing straw in aimless
circles in a barn. There is a feeling
in this farmhouse not so much of exile
as of stasis, as though the creaking
floorboards and ancient wood
stove cannot assert themselves.
At the church cemetery two maples
cast shadows across the marker
where he stands, and he puts his hands
in his pockets and wonders how much longer
he should wait there, these visits
like the drunk who clutches the empty
bottle to his chest, or like indifferent
light that falls through kitchen windows
in the winter. No one whispers any longer.
The cows low late at night. What pours
out of him is barren as a soybean field
in February, when the ground is frozen stiff
beneath your boots, and the snow at dusk
looks gray as ash as it is falling.

Sunday Mornings

This is the sound of polished shoes
and Sunday mornings. Of August cornfields,
their arms raised in supplication.
Of pond water congealing into muck—
slow summers in languishing abeyance.
My brother and I rise each day and hold
ourselves suspended; we hide in empty
spaces between heartbeats. We watch
the gathering reds and golds ride like sorrow
on cloud underbellies. Our father's
tractor chugs and expels black smoke.
We have gone this way before. We walk
the fields and sense the air grow still.
The day shimmers and reclaims us.
Our flesh is weak. I lie on straw and feel
the grief flee out of me. These are prayers
of dirt, of rich loam we fear will bury us.
We listen to the inland prairie sea, to waves
of wind that scar the land, to our mother
weeping down the hall. The heat hangs
heavy as a noose. The cows low
late at night. In our worst dreams
our father's hands and feet turn black.
They caw like crows then disappear
beyond the field. This air is rich
with tallgrass and manure. The walls can't
absorb what I am feeling. This ancient
house crumbles with its age. Bricks fall.
Pipes burst. Plaster chips and scatters.
My brother cries soundlessly for our
father. Each Sunday the pews are hard
as flint. Hymns rise to the rafters
and beyond. Every sermon is preverbal, as raw
as grit. When church is over, the four of
us walk out into the heat. Sunday's done.
Only chores are left. We strip off shirts—

our father's scar puckers in the sun and draws
a map. In the pond a bloated dead
raccoon floats—the blueflies are ravenous
with greed. Old farms have soil like a
graveyard. You feel it in your fingers, taste it.
It is the weight of generations. The church
cemetery is visible from our barn. We stand
there in the midday sun—baked in dizziness.
Heat empties out the soul. At the funeral
home I reach into the open casket.
Our father has retreated inside his skin.
His eyes are closed. It is Sunday. Nothing
swims in our back pond. The hours congeal
as weight, as translation of memory,
as instruments of what we do not know. The rain
won't fall. The earth peels like rotting skin.
The cistern is blank as a dead eye. This is
the sound of polished shoes. Of August corn.
Of arms reaching out in supplication.

Confetti

In Wilgus County in Northern Minnesota,
two brothers row out on Lake Elizabeth at dusk,
their ties clinging stiffly to their throats, the air steamy.
The peeper frogs whisper their secrets
as the older brother leans his weight into the oars,
and the liquid universe swells and dips beneath them.

Back on shore, their mother's house is dark,
though the fields, those eternal stalks,
lift like a blessing toward the gathering twilight.
And inside her house there is a photograph by the fireplace.
She is skinny-legged and freckled in a cornfield,
captured perfectly in childhood,
a dream concealed deep inside a memory.

She used to tell them stories about her grandfather,
who lived by that same lake and one time hid inside a field
as Objibwe Indians set the barn ablaze.
Memories are blazes, too, of course, the torch of years,
her grandfather crouching low and fearful amid the corn,
their mother kneeling like a prayer inside her garden,
her hands like keepsakes in the fertile earth,
the smoldering gray of Lake Elizabeth behind her.

It is confetti, the younger brother thinks, despite himself,
as the urn comes open and is offered to the wind,
and the ashes take flight—fluttering like recollections.

And a moment later something rises from the shallows,
a great blue heron, lifting itself on awkward wings,
claiming the gathering sky, the deepening reds and golds,
and beats a path above the rocking boat.

Eventide

He used to ride the bus on Saturdays to Comal County.
He wasn't married any longer, and his son had last
sent a letter from Abilene the summer he turned fourteen.
It wasn't just because of the Guadalupe River
he would go. He liked to think he was carrying
some unknown part of himself into the hill country.
He couldn't say why or how he'd come not to know it,
and he certainly never thought he might unearth it
on the trip. What he imagined was himself standing
on the banks of that old river and looking up at the steep
limestone cliffs. What he imagined was himself
leaning against a basswood or persimmon tree—
and maybe he'd spot an armadillo or white-tailed deer
moving like a ghost or dream so high up. Back when
he was drinking he took his son there once and lost him
for an hour on a hiking trail, but he never thought
he went back there looking for the boy—as though
you could reclaim memory like that. He knew
about loss. He was okay with it. He took the bus
just so he could stand there for a time and look around.
Or maybe he'd wade in the river to his knees. Then he'd
ride the bus back home at eventide. It was the best part
of the day. He could sit there above the world,
wondering what thing of him he'd left behind.

VI

Teaching the Gods to Breathe

They must have begun immortality in stasis,
the ether like a mist or morning deer standing still
amid the cordgrass. There was no wind
to lift the air and help it breathe. The eternal
sleeping lake must have been splashed with light
so pale it could not cling, even to the gray—
like on the morning we stepped beneath
the tent flap and waded out into the prairie.
Surely the gods sense the essence of a thing,
like tickseed and purple coneflowers close to bloom,
and know to elongate each moment into clarity.
Then to breathe in suddenly as the wind picks up,
the deer leaps off into the bluestem,
and the great blue heron rises from the lake.

Hillside Wraith

There is a moment after you regret
what you have done, when the veil
of otherness encloses you and all you feel
is disconnected from your bones.
      Like the time his mother
slapped him. He was twelve. Sneaking
from his bedroom window, he
rowed on Cattail Pond and watched
the raindrops forming pockmarks
in the shallows.
      And the night before they buried her—
his own son then was almost six—
she came to him after midnight in a dream.
The family existed then as hills exist. The moon
stood tumbled and weighty on the ridge.
And he sensed her there
as pockmarks in a pond.

The Known World

The train rises on the ridge behind
the house. He hears it in the darkness
and thinks of the intensity of fields
as snow is falling. The snow that fell
when he was younger was voiceless as the woods
behind the creek, and the white flakes that
clung nightly to his coat and hair
were ghostly in the treetops.
He has come to think that memories
are like teenage lovers
meeting secretly in winter, the snow
falling soundlessly around them,
their tender mouths—bruised
yet eager—wordless as the sky.
And then, at once, a train appears above a ridge—
and they both turn. The light bears down
along the tracks. A horn cries out.
And the known world trembles to be heard.

The Water in Between

Only when they climbed out on the island rocks
and glanced back at the white shuttered house,
their mother's green tomatoes on the vine,
the formless Lake Lucy in between,
did they gaze up at their bedroom window
and imagine they were waiting in the shadows.
Years later the older brother would thumb
through wedding photographs
to read in Margaret's eyes why she had left him.
And the younger brother would rock slowly
in his dead son's school yard swing.
How did we swim so far? we ask the watery sunlight.
Then a green wave lifts itself and falls,
leaving only whatever lies between.

The Myth of Ice

My father's pale pink knees bob like floating ice
beneath the steering wheel. His breath,
heavy as plowed snowdrifts, blurs the windshield
glass before my face, making January streets
ethereal as mist. I am plunged into sensation.
My father's tennis racket a songless lyre in back.
My mother's driveway emerging from the ether.
I am home. It is the myth of ice that emotions
like molecules slow down, crystallize, then stop.
That weekends at my father's remain in stasis.
His car slides off and I imagine him skating
on his indoor court of green, while I, encased
these past three days in a sleek cocoon of ice,
am compressed down to emotions dense as stone.

VII

Black Tupelo Country

Down amid the bottomlands,
                    where the backwater woods
reshuffle themselves from stuporous summer
into fall,
                    these black tupelos
and their deep blue fruit make a salve
                    to fend off ghosts.
And beneath the flickering, wind-trembling canopy,
                    pileated woodpeckers
batter out their secret message to the invisible.
                    A message
that old man Llewellyn, dying in his cabin since July,
half-hears inside a dream
                    of a speckled king snake swallowing
a mouse head first. Dreams like these, as he knows,
are trying to carry him
                    into the belly of the infinite.
And though his wife and sister and grandchildren
make a potion of corydalis, wild buttercup, and larkspur,
he sees the world
                    dimming transparent all around him,
transparent as the moonlit view from the pond bottom
                    amid the cattail stalks.
And too soon, he believes, the black tupelo will lift him
                    in its inexorable arms,
and its lapis-lazuli-blue berries will fade paler
                    and paler
until his skin falls as loose as the king snake's—
then the pileated woodpecker will
                    sound the funeral drum,
and only the black tupelo salve smeared
                    out of familial mercy
on his stilled chest will prevent his released spirit
from swooping beneath
                    the wind-moaning canopy.

Beneath the Shagbark

It began with a strange roughness to his skin,
a rash along his ribs. He made a salve
of pennyworts and featherfoils, but soon
mole crickets began crawling in his hair,
pomace flies emerging from hidden furrows
of his flesh, leafhoppers waiting trapped inside his nostrils.
When his teeth came loose what grew in their stead
were gnarled roots and furry catkins. Sometimes
he peeled his skin like bark and his hair grew wild
as shoots along his arms. He lay awake nights
and imagined vegetable marrow throbbing
through his veins, black loam sifting deep
into his belly. Lying back, he listened to the wind
and watched the first celadine come clawing
in slow motion from his chest. Next the monkshood
grew, the wild columbine, the checkerberry, the fireweed.
A copse of split-gilled mushrooms appeared along
what used to be his legs. It was lonely, then—
until two deer came walking one dusk beneath
the shagbark, dropped their heads, and ate.

Black Water

All at once it's October night again. Clouds
devolving as cataracts above Squawroot Lake.
The tied-off rowboat
                         bumping and grieving against the pilings.
Strong winds
             rippling across the black water, lifting and finding
me at the upstairs window.
                    Something's coming. I can sense it
in the back-yard beech tree's leaves,
                         twitching like epileptics.
I can feel it in the dark runnel of cold seeping
through the screen mesh, reminding me
of a bottomlands story
                    of a young woman who fell from the sky
in late autumn. Was found by two reclusive brothers
collecting wood for gathering winter.
In one version she was found
                 in a bear den,
in another by the shores of Squawroot Lake.
But in every version she was dead when they found her,
dead until they touched her
                 and she stood again as upright bones.
She was beautiful, supposedly, which meant the brothers
couldn't help but be in love.
In one version they brought her back to their cabin,
vied for her affections, and eventually
                         disassembled each other
with their axes. In another she bore them a death-child
who grew up, surveyed the situation, and
                     drowned them all.
Which is what the wind says tonight, I'm afraid,
as it comes pouring across
                 the black water. Lashing
through the screen mesh. Whispering

                              of the blunt blade,
of self-oblivion, of death in life, of deep-measured
winter, and of quivering
                    unworkable love.

Ouroboros

That February in our tupelo bottomlands,
                              two-hundred
canebrake rattlesnakes were unearthed hibernating
in the rocky crevices behind the old
                    Missionary Baptist Church.
Discovered dreaming, the rattlesnakes, curled and reclusive
                              in their pell-mell multitudes.
Dreaming, my grandfather told us, of ouroboros,
tail-swallower, eater of the eternal, self-devourer.
                         Shaded, those snakes,
in a coppery, feathery twilight
seeping into the rocky narrows before igniting into flames.
          Igniting when the Hauk brothers doused in
the gasoline and flung the match.
                              Spring brought the voles,
shrews, chipmunks, deer mice, squirrels, cotton rats,
                         and oracle moles.
Crawling, blossoming, chaotic throngs of them
that no amount of toothwort or woodbine
would scare away. Then Pastor Reverend Otis Lowell's
young wife had her miscarriage
and the older Hauk brother fell from the barn roof
and snapped his neck.
                    So when my grandfather,
Bumpa—who first told us the story—
traveled north to bury his last sister
and stepped outside after dark one night and saw
                         the aurora borealis
undulating flickering above the Minnesota prairie,
saw the spectral green phosphorescent
                    strands of light writhing,
he knew then where all those sleeping, dying,
tail-swallowing canebrakes
had gone to burn.

Ice Junco

The bird is frozen in the ice. Black and frozen
in ice that will not scrape—not even when he claws
it with a stick. Later he will imagine its eyes
as red, or thunderhead gray, or sooty white.
He will be doing homework after school,
or eating dinner at the kitchen table, and every
sound he hears is *junco, junco*. As though
his bird is singing from the ice. And some nights
in his dreams when the snow comes drifting
upward from the stream, rising like an apparition
past his window, he imagines it's not snow at all
but juncos, white juncos, small as horseflies, fluttering.
And sometimes when the train cries out from the ridge
beyond the barn—he imagines juncos swooping
down like bats, or he pictures fish thawing and wiggling
inside ice. And mornings when he hurries down to the creek
beyond the barn—where the shagbark leaves crunch
beneath his boots—he is eager to discover if the stream
is trickling once more into the drainage ditch,
if the ice is scattered and broken in the mud.
In which case he will bend to poke his junco
with a stick. And either it will quiver or it won't.

Dressing the Dead

Her limbs resist him on the embalming table
and seem almost to flail.
She defies him with the cool radiance
of her skin. He refuses to watch her red hair
flame as he is scrubbing her—refuses
to recall her by the river,
swimming with her brother in the cattails.
Her long hair writhing like a cottonmouth.
Last summer he leaned against the crematory,
watched her step from her house,
her infant daughter in one arm.
She looked up, saw him, waved—
so that night he mixed milk vetch,
bittersweet, motherwort, trumpet creepers.
And dreamed that ash was falling
in the river where she swam.
Come fall he kept a five-lined skink
inside his pocket—at the cemetery
he prayed he'd never hear
the steady drip that he hears now.
When she is drained he pierces her
with the trocar—her opened eyes
besiege him in their blankness.
And not until he dresses her,
covers the bruises on her cheeks
and chin and neck,
inserts the eye caps, lifts her
to the gurney, ties
her hands and feet with string,
and wheels her to the Reposing Room,
does she finally seem at ease
with what's been done.
So he steps out back
and walks down to the river.

Does not lift his eyes to the brother's house.
Sits on the frozen bank
until the snow begins to fall.

Bottomlands Widow

Fire blight has infected her apple trees again.
The milky ooze drips like stigmata
from the infected blossoms. In her dream
she slices into the entrails of a musk turtle,
and what she finds—finds inside the apple-white flesh—
is something living, something pulpy and soggy
with blood, a girl child. After her husband died
she imagined for a time that she was pregnant.
In the woods she gathered bitter bolete,
rattlesnake plantains, goat's rue. Her dream child
was as small as a fist. She heard once that birds
when they died became bats, which explained
their frenzied flight, their hinged wings.
Once her husband shot a doe and dragged it back
to the house. She was watching from the window
as he knelt down with the hunting knife.
She used to wonder as a child what kept the moon
from sliding on the clouds, what kept the stars impaled
so they wouldn't slip. Her husband slipped the knife
into the swollen belly. She was watching from the window.
This evening her apple trees are bleeding, and rain drips
like stigmata from the sky. The hoot owl cries out
in her husband's voice and shames her. She has no choice.
It shames her to say she is happy.

VIII

Weed Song

Like that bicycle that came weaving
once into the busy intersection,

riderless as a wobbly apparition.
Or that jar of formalin my uncle kept

for decades in his cellar, hiding something
listing, pulpy, mysterious inside.

Or the heart and body separated, divided
like fence slats, or crows in the evening—

while dusk is blackening beyond the elms
and dandelions, bright as egg yolks, dim.

No Other Sign

This, then, is how they teach us to begin.
We were standing on the railroad platform
in August sunlight. We were trying
to remember. Your train was late.
The night before, the fires in the hills
behind our apartment house filled the window
with a pale and otherworldly orange. We watched
until our bodies fell asleep. I dreamed that smoke
came drifting down the canyon and whispered
through the screen mesh. This was not
the spirit dying. This was more the way
that light falls across the surface of a lake—
then shatters into pieces that catch fire.
In the morning as I drove you to the station,
I remembered reading how the Emperor Xuanzong
missed his dead wife so much he tried
to find her in the spirit world, and that Taoists
believe it is possible to transform yourself
into water by standing near a lake, transform yourself
into fire by standing near a fire. After your train
was gone, I drove far into the hills to smell the smoke.

The Return

He returns to the river where once he waded
through the cattails, where surrounding soybean fields
turned yellow as prophecy each Michigan summer.
As a boy he waded through the milkweeds,
the jimsonweeds, the dogbanes. He sat on the railroad
tracks while twilight was folding back behind
the house and watched the distant heat lightning—
until the ache hollowed out his bones. He knew little
then about the way a landscape enters the body
and couldn't imagine being drawn back some day
to stand where the tree roots sketched their skeletons
on the muddy river bank, where the blessing
of dusk glowed bare, raw, and empty in the fields—
light lifting into the dimming copper sky.

Distant Trees

This is said to be the hopeful time
of day: dawn whispering in the poplars,
stars and moon
                        unraveling like thread
out of the needle.
We put the best face on it:
low-slung clouds drooping,
                        sluggish rivers vanishing.
But then the alarm clock bleats
like a gutted goat and the trucks
out on the highway rattle by
                        like grinding stones.
And the dull disregard that follows
us from bed, that follows us as we slip
into our trousers, that follows as we knot our ties—
sags into the hollow of our bellies.
And in the bathroom mirror,
spitting mouthwash, dulled and impassive,
blank and bloodless, our swollen
                        faces ache.

IX

Here Is What I Know about the Sky

My brother is standing on the barn roof, shooting at gravestones across Old State Route 17. If it were Sunday, organ music might be welling up from the hardscrabble Baptist church atop our hill, welling up into the raw November air. If it were Monday, we might be bouncing and swaying in our Wilgus County school bus, our books held with practiced indifference in our laps. But it's Saturday, and it's a Marlin .22 he keeps shooting, a single shot, which means he spends most of his time reloading. I hear the sound of the bolt as it snaps back into place. I hear the sound of the shot, and it's as though another tiny hole has been opened in the fabric of the day. And every time—even though I know with certainty it's coming, even though I feel it coming—I always look up. And here's the thing: the pigs I'm feeding always look up, too.

It's that deaf boy related to Frank Thompson from Convoy who hangs himself. The boy is two years older than me and lives above the downtown post office with his uncle. He hangs himself from a basswood limb across the street from the high school where eventually I'll go. No one finds him hanging there until morning. A girl named Julie Stolis is the one who sees him when she's walking to school past the old softball field, so when I close my eyes I always see Julie first, and then I see the deaf boy hanging, and then I see the morning sky peering out above the softball field.

It's my grandfather on my father's side who tells us that dead birds—robins, sparrows, bluejays, woodpeckers, you name it—come back to life as bats. I know this isn't true, but when I watch them swarming nights beneath our maples, zigzagging nights like falling chips of broken sky, I always look up into the blackness and reconsider.

One day when I am older I will meet a woman whose former husband died in a plane crash in South Carolina. It happened a long time ago, she will tell me, and though she will be naked before she says it, she will cover herself with the sheet as she speaks the words, which I will well understand and not begrudge, especially since the sheet will come off again when she is done. More important, in my mind, will be the way I will see her watching airplanes every time we are out walking by the Burdock River. Not a lot of planes will pass that far out in the country, but when they do she will always look up—every time—and I will always imagine she is half-expecting to see this one fall.

Any second he will shoot again—that's what I'm thinking in my head. After all, the bolt just went. After all, I can feel it. Without looking up, I can picture my brother standing on the barn roof, standing there against the morning sky. I won't actually hear the bullet whistling overhead, of course, but whistle overhead it probably will. Something moving that fast must surely whistle, I believe. And though it's hard to imagine, it will exist above me for the smallest fraction of a second before it goes thunking into the dirt across the road.

And that's all I know about the sky.

Speaking of Rivers

A man in a bar speaks of rivers. Not of swathers,
sickle bar mowers, square balers, front end loaders,
sorghum, soybeans. In prairie towns like this, bar stools
are hard as church pews and the only river most farmers
speak about is the Mad River. The man's boy,
age ten, waits impatiently for his father to stop talking.
The boy's eyes are closed and he tries not to hear his father's
thickened words: Breg, Salzach, Lech, Danube, Elbe,
Spree, Brigach, Leine, Oder, Warnow, Schwentine, Rhine.
His accent returns to his childhood as he drinks.
Like at the cemetery two years earlier, when German words
came pouring out in moans. The boy wishes he could
forget his father kneeling on the cemetery grass. Raw earth.
Green stains on his father's best slacks. Indeed, twenty years
later he would think of Orpheus begging Zeus to save
Eurydice—then losing everything twice. He would recall
his mother helping his father with his collecting: monarchs,
buckeyes, crescents, great spangled fritillaries, anglewings,
red admirals, tortoise shells, mourning cloaks, viceroys,
admirals, wood nymphs, blues, gray hairstreaks,
snouts, sulphurs, swallowtails. Like Christ on the cross,
pinned like a butterfly by the thorax, his mother's orange
hair clinging to a brush in the bathroom a week after
she was covered by the dirt. Like Orpheus singing mournful
songs on his lyre. Or a father's drunken lonely voice
in a bar while his child drinks grape soda. Fulda River.
Saale, Ruwer, Volme. Words endless as rain battering
a tavern's tin roof. A mouth wide as bare earth as
they lower in a coffin. Words running, dancing, skipping—
and loitering in bars. Words holy as pig manure on boot bottoms.
Words baked like sunlit soybean fields. Words forever
guttural and foreign. Every river speaking in moans.

Desire

It was as though he had fallen asleep again on a park bench
in his German-American neighborhood when he was nine.
And as he slept he heard breaking glass and someone starting
a bonfire in the bushes. In the dream black storm clouds
loomed above the small pond and its smaller copse of trees,
though they loomed with a certain luridness he liked, a sexy
luridness, he decided, not then but later, much later, and soon
in the dream rain began to fall around him in great and
thumping drops, as though the drops had something pleasant on
their mind, though he didn't know what, and suddenly he saw
himself as an adult leaning out of a hotel balcony in Berlin or
Munich or Cologne, true German cities, while a true German
Fräulein in the room behind him removed a silk dress and hung
it neatly on the chair—then winked when he turned to her,
winked in a way that struck him as strange though nicely lurid,
lurid even as the rain, lurid even as the bonfire, lurid even as
breaking glass, all of which he understood as his desire.

Bottomlands Memory, 1927

He had chopped wood for her all month. Ever since the husband
had gone to stay with a dying father in Atlanta. Mornings when
he arrived at Buford Swamp, the mist seeped like a premonition
through the black tupelos. *Here are your pale clothes*, the river seemed
to say, *here are your gray garments*. He had come to imagine the land
around her cabin as filled with sacred objects: the flickering yel-
low of the prothonotary warbler, the waterlily seeds floating as an
augury in the current, the cottonmouths muscling primitive through
the pickerelweeds. Some days his body shuddered to see her on the
front porch with her children. Some days he left the splintered logs
as an offering at her feet. As a school boy in Wiesbaden he had read
Die Leiden des jungen Werthers, and now nights he wrote letters home
to his mother about the forlorn feeling of an axe handle in a palm,
about the loneliness of the anhinga stretching its wings on shore or
swimming with just its snake-like head above the river. Years later
the memory would be reduced to that: what poured out in an episto-
lary fever. Smudged, German syllables wept across a page. A life's
lacking borne into eternity by candlelight.

X

Four Hooves and the Goat to Go with Them

Exiled from the Garden, E. and A. sold
submarine sandwiches at the strip mall.
Poor A.'s asthma was worsened by the apples
rotting and fermenting in their back yard.
They bought a goat and imagined offering
it as sacrifice, but instead they fed it chocolate
chip pancakes and tossed a rubber ball
it finally ate. This was the same summer
A. broke his ribs and afterwards was hooked
for months on Vicodin. Evenings they sat
on their tiny porch and watched the sun
sink behind the refinery, and once E. spotted
a mist of insects hovering like a forgotten hand
near her tomato plants. Another time they saw
on television a giant anaconda swallow a goat,
and later that night E. kissed A.'s Adam's apple
while he was sleeping. For their anniversary
they made love naked in the yard—while the goat
chewed the grass as sacrament, while
the mosquitoes anointed them in blood.

Retirement Years

After finally returning to Ithaca, O. bought a partial interest in
a Cinnabon. It was strange to pass his days at a shopping mall,
to watch the crowds mulling all around him, to feel his old bones
ache and the sea no longer sway and list beneath him. Often as
he went wandering past The Gap or Old Navy or Radio Shack,
he marveled at how much his life had changed, and each time he
stood behind the cash register he couldn't fathom how the salty
air was now the smell of sticky buns. And while P. stayed home
most days to watch her soaps, O. was restless. The sound of
garbage trucks chased him from bed each day before first light.
And after work when he stopped at The Lotus-Eaters Inn, the
beer was flat and stale, the barmaids were homely as Polyphe-
mus, and his fellow patrons were as tiresome as those suitors of
P.'s he'd had to kill. Often late at night he dreamed he was talk-
ing to the dead, but they didn't have much to say, and even when
he bought a ram on eBay he couldn't bring himself to slaughter
it, not when it gazed at him with such rheumy eyes. More and
more he began imagining sneaking Circe's secret potion into
the Cinnabon dough, but already half his customers were fat as
swine, and in any case he no longer saw the point. So what if
the mannequins at Victoria's Secret reminded him faintly of the
Sirens? There was little point in being lashed to any mast. He
was past all that. He was washed up. Too often at the end of
the day he walked out into the parking lot and wept. And when
his birthday came and P. bought him a dog, it was more than he
could bear. A profound melancholy gripped him as he locked
himself in the bathroom and sat on the bathtub rim. *Poor lost
Argos*, he thought. *Poor lost me.* Everything finally came to ruin.
And all that awaited were those dark rivers of the Underworld.

Epistemology in Cleveland

In his final years Socrates was living on the streets down by the river. He slept beneath the underpass, and the smell of exhaust fumes became for him a kind of synesthesia. Each passing bus played in his head its Divine chord of Piety or Mysticism or Eros, and each truck lumbering, thudding across the metal grating announced viscerally the Soul's first Bodily Incarnation. Sometimes at first light he checked the dumpsters outside of Wal-Mart, and often he stepped inside and engaged the Greeter in a Dialogue. Was there a difference, he would ask, between Injuring people and Wronging them? Was Ignorance in itself an Evil? The odd looks he received deterred him from talking to the children at the school yard by which he pushed his shopping cart at noon, and the glances from the teachers often seemed more bitter even than the Hemlock. Yet only sometimes did he recall Xanthippe, Lamprocles, Sophroniscus, and Menexenus. Was it not, he daily spoke aloud, that if a thing has less of Truth it also has less of real essence and existence? Occasionally a passerby would press Epistemological coins into his hands, and the weight of them and their impression was as wondrous as the Eleusinian Mysteries themselves.

Blue Toaster

In the final summer of his life
Dr. Mengele took a job as a Greeter
at a Wal-Mart in Miami.
He rented a small room above a bodega.
In the evenings he read *The Aeneid*
or took a bus to the beach
so he could stand in the sand slathered
with sunscreen and watch the waves
grow slowly gray then disappear.
For a short time he kept a dream journal,
expecting to write about gypsies,
dwarves, twins, Jews, castration,
transfusions, sex changes, and surgeries;
but instead he dreamed each night
of a shy shop girl he'd adored when he was
a young boy at the Günzburg Gymnasium,
or about the blue toaster he had bought
a few days earlier with his employee discount
at Wal-Mart, or about how much his long
lost son, Rolf, would have liked the French fries
at McDonald's or the salsa music
that always seemed to be vibrating
against his apartment window after midnight.
Only for a brief while did he collect
assassin bugs in pickle jars to see
how they would respond to being left
on his baking window sill at noon;
but eventually he let them go and drank
an American beer and listened
to the Florida Marlins on the radio.
At work he learned to smile and nod
as each customer arrived through
the automatic doors. It was a small miracle,
he thought. The doors whooshed open

and there they were. And only sometimes
did he recall the railhead at Auschwitz
where he would point each prisoner
to the left or to the right. Now he pointed
toward the appliance section or maybe to the toys.
And small children occasionally
ran up to hold his hand.

The Body Art of Frederik Ruysch

Come, see, judge,
believe only your own eyes:
a bright tortoise egg
in a child's amputated hand.
A fetus decked out in a collar
and a cap. The body's struggle
to resurrect itself.
Look: a four-hundred-
year-old sun is animating
dust motes above an embryo
in the jaws of a stilled snake
from the Dark Continent.
Come see our repository of curiosities:
bodies sliding effortlessly
between subject and object,
slippers constructed
from human skin.
A wondrous freak show
of festooned skeletons,
dioramas of body parts,
"living" and beautified cadavers.
Vene, vidi et judica nil tuis oculus.
And finally at his hand-carved
work table—the hands rubbed raw
from resin, balsamicus,
white wax, and cinnabar—
our long-dead anatomist,
our praelector, our artist,
our husband, and our father—
slipping another child
into a jar.

XI

Disfigured Night

This dim gray cloth of morning
is lifting itself from the pickerelweeds.
And here is the world's shape.
Not only broken vessels
sinking after midnight into the cypress swamp.
The rhythmic pull dragging us
beneath the sweetgum trees.
                              The neighbor boys
were in our bottomlands
again last night. Shooting, we imagine,
at the black tupelos. Buckshot scattering
everywhere as hollowed fruit.
Like that thin-ribbed bobcat we saw once
dragging a dead rope
of a plain-bellied water snake
into the possumhaw. A dead rope
twisting anyway as an unwilling occultation.
                              It was disfigured night
when we awoke, plucked and blindfolded
in bed, and the windows shook
and jerked us to our feet.
From our back porch we divined
ourselves as what hides beyond the bladderwort,
as Spanish moss left hanging
in the trees.

Symmetry

One imagines a reliquary of cottonmouth
skins and black bear claws, or mason

jars dark in the cellar with the entrails
of pickerel frogs, ground up chicken turtle

shells, vulture beaks and feathers.
Or the symmetry of possumhaw

and swamp lilies carried in wet clumps
to our grandmother's kitchen to be ground

into a salve. Or here amid the lanceolate leaves
and the pale flowers borne on catkins,

the crown gall black as disfigured tumors,
as mummified rot, sagging the branches

of the same black willow from which
our grandmother harvested so long ago

the bitter bark to steep in tea and soothe
our aches and fevers.

Bird, Branch

What is waiting in the cypress swamp
is an occultation. The hushed voices
of wind stirring through the sweetgum trees,
the black willows, the possumhaws.
The red-bellied water snake writhing
like a premonition through the bladderwort.
Think of musk turtles secreting their yellowish
stench beside the pickerelweeds, my brother
plucking a wood duck then tossing
the bloodied feathers into the epidendrums.
And beside us in the river the cottonmouths
are whispering their augury: the vertical slits
of pupils, the pocked and pitted cheeks,
the hollowed fangs sharp as stalactites.
Childhood settling again like a prothonotary
warbler on a tupelo limb—while blood-red
morning fills the swamp.

The Marriage

Think of the way the blackjack oak
and its twisted limbs stand in stark relief against
the falling snow. Or in summer how the toads eat
the spilled dog food on the patio.
His grandmother used to whisper that fireweeds
could be ground into a potion for fertility.
She believed that the young rose-colored
leaves of the wisteria could be smeared against your skin
to ward off death. And in his dream at night he is standing
in a field besieged by insects. There are click beetles,
scarab beetles, leafhoppers, assassin bugs, and vespid wasps.
He is not alone—he senses it. He knows her shadow
is cast against the reedgrass. Or imagine a Sunday hymn
that rises to the church rafters and lingers there.
Like that. Like Jesus healing ten lepers
but only the one Samaritan comes back to thank him.
Or the catfish writhing and twisting after church
like an epileptic on the dock. Here is the wedding dance,
some think. Here is the sacrament. He remembers
falling once as a child from a rowboat into the lake.
Like that. Like the reeds twisting around your legs.
His grandfather taught him to slip the knife
into the entrails of the leopard frog. To wade
into the brackish marshes. It's the smell.
It's the sound of the eastern diamondback
by the saw-palmettos. It's those toads.
Having their fill.

Stationary Darkness

One thinks of apparitional black willows and tupelos
smudging beyond the pickerelweeds. Of summer air

steeping into the cypress swamp. Of twilight dimming
as Abraham's hopes as he bound Isaac with the last

rope to the altar. Surely we know to love and hate
the humped and airless mountain ridges rolling their way

into the infinite. The smell of God infusing the marbled
clouds with the burnt offering. Imagine a single moment

slowing or even stopping above the bottomlands.
The molecules congealing like the green muck into which

the alligator snapping turtle slides. This is the final
reckoning and love. The last moment before the Spanish

moss drapes the possumhaw in stationary darkness.
Glassy light clinging to the sacrificial blade.

Ritual Cloud Line

August Sunday. Pale smoke rising from the burning
tupelo stump. Unrolling premonition
                                        beneath the cloud line.
When all at once my younger brother, Raymond, steps
beside me on the front porch. His hands propped
                                        in his pockets.
And both of us simply stand there,
                                        watching.

More than twelve hours have elapsed
since we first drilled the holes. Since our father dropped in the
                                        saltpeter.
Since we lit the fire and watched the smoke begin to
                                        drift
like a dark divination above the bottomlands.

And whatever it is we imagine is smoldering there
inside the stump, transmogrifying
                                        to smoke and ash,
seeping like some dark
                                        augury
into the sky, we've always known that it would find us.
If not here then in the hoot owl's cry. In the snake-twitch
                                        of the tall grass.
In the amanitas or spectral moon-glow
                                        at midnight.
In the ritual cloud lines of bottom-heavy storms.
In the human
                                        paroxysm.
In the future pirouetting on the fang's edge
or root-ravaged in the loam.

All pouring from a burning
                                        tupelo stump.

Doug Ramspeck coordinates the Writing Center at The Ohio State University at Lima, where he also teaches English. Since he began writing poems in 2004, his work has appeared in over two hundred publications, including *Passages North*, *West Branch*, and *Hayden's Ferry*. A graduate of Kenyon College and the University of California at Irvine, he lives in Lima with his wife, Beth Sutton-Ramspeck, and their daughter, Lee. *Black Tupelo Country* is his first book.